Erec & Enide

Amy De'Ath was born in Suffolk in 1985. She studied at the University of East Anglia and in Philadelphia, US, before moving to Australia and then to London. Her poems have appeared in a wide variety of journals in the UK and US and will feature in the *Salt Younger Poets 2011* anthology. She currently lives and works in London, and is Poet-in-Residence at the University of Surrey. This is her first book of poems.

I0087967

Erec & Enide

by

Amy De'Ath

SALT

LONDON

PUBLISHED BY SALT PUBLISHING
Dutch House, 307–308 High Holborn, London WC1V 7LL United Kingdom

Salt Publishing 2010

Printed and bound in the United Kingdom by Lightning Source UK Ltd

Typeset in Swift 9.5 / 13

ISBN 978 1 84471 809 2 paperback

1 3 5 7 9 8 6 4 2

for my parents,

Sue & Paul De'Ath

Contents

Acknowledgements

Earlier versions of some of these poems have appeared in
Esque, The Rialto, Signals, Spine and *Quid.*

Thanks and love to my friends and family. I am especially
grateful to Amy King, Ana Božičević, Daniel Kane, Tim Atkins,
Jonathan Styles and Peter Gizzi for their art, friendship and
kind encouragement.

Above all, thank you to 'Erec'. My *line of flight.*

'Thou was my truft in my Youth'

Poetry for Boys

That the Joy will soon come and make you suffer!

Lay low in the words of the wood,
very subtle, not immune,
lay down in the snow and incline,
you are rest enough and dowry,
in the lay and the spook of an age,
very poor, still glamour,
still further than you think even
more, from the day duly swallow,
to the real green day in the dream,
very full, cracking bough,
the undoing publicity of meaning
all the whole black sky is feeling
the screwing over, resin delight
delightful residual meaning, still night.

I'm a weeping boy and a centaur caving in.
Adventures, find me—I'm hard to come by.
In the days when mirrors were made of burnished silver
I stayed up late,
in the nearly beautiful night I stood not quite
in the shower plenty natural and the water washed into
the time of my skin.
I imagined how to answer the question of whether
psychic malady is a personal affair. Then I wrung
my hair and dye came out.

If I had the money to dip in being a boy,
if I was Anna O., & fallen into autism or
steeped in prelingual glimpses of Lena's face,
I'd be living system: looped in my own elements.

A system closing talking only to itself.

III

The house is full of dehumidifiers. Behind the house
a warm damp world enlarges itself, puffs
leaves and shelled birdsong along in it, and a baby crying
and deeds of courage.

If the sea is the swan road you can
appropriate the lake-lady just by laughing.
You don't have to bed her to make her love you.
The ivy thinks it's English:
a swish of ermine reveals the last girl standing, and
she is sugary and she is foxy and maybe she is Jewish.
She swims the channel towards your parinage.

How will she mark her scent?
She's sleepy and reaches land and regulatory forest. She's sleepy.
Her leaf-hair trails behind her with crisp packets.
How will she tend the steer?
How will she steer the wheel?

IV

There is a boy who (I) cannot lose,
unbridled is he and of real flesh
by Spanish radio he and I were made to be
And I, he not made nor ever been,
nor ever did I went with he, never
eat by such great lies or lied with
great intent, did I swim swim again
or consider praying men then give
my heart to all the boy in pasta—

O, hold me in the light.

v

I turned 25 and my conception finished:
Is my face
already the death-mask, yes?
And not featuring lakes much anymore
and notwithstanding the 21st century,
and sitting, watching East Anglia shudder and insisting
never to have been an Angle!

Is a boy only happening
like this: carving out tuning forks
amenable sausage
recycled lovecats, acts of love,
a wireless odour of US coast,
its vintage blushing
overblown: yes, it's a boy

and I am a boy now applauding myself on the wet grass.
I give myself a peppered kiss.
I love the visionary earth-boys by diluted petty means like this.

VI

Here we go, my legs blow back
into the garden, the latest late-night
cicada store is so appealing I know
I will stay here 'til humanity ends.

Well it's tough, the greatest fish
mow close to the coral and
the friendliest cats say 'hi' a million
as they slap your ass.

Say I stay, open-legged for the
summer, feet stuck firmly in the
Airtrain, a dewy idea peaking at what
Is this vector I caress?
What ran my legs brushing
alongside the linotype, O Walty,
Won't you sidle or trot smartly by
me, you are just a dog,
You don't know what it's like.

[6]

Down dampen sully unknown
because you ate the sunshine,
asunder among the porch-light
a tune to know, of history's mesh
an epistolary flash of deer
young, always in fashion, in brave
pursuit, climbing down a piece
of fruit to get to the last boy in
town, who ate the town and
whipped his jacket up to the
wind and ripened on a cloud,
a compensating cloud in glut, and
he fell down, he fell upon those
vandals, he was a feat of sunshine.

VIII

Boys and solipsists are written out and I pant for boys in
appellatives, I'd eat your hair and holes my God.

I call them puissant debtors and lavish roadies
or whatever you want.

I sleep in nature where warrens
serve as nail bars

I'm a stubborn boy and poised
at that beat replaced in love.

wherever my body takes precedence
I do not owe a boy, either.

it's like this forever

. . .

Wherever I am, Hello boy.
I do not owe a law, either.

Dreamboat

I think a melting slope is a cliché intended as a lure;
I want to grab my younger selves by the collars and
archive them.

I want every boat to turn its prow toward me.
I feel the cure is just around the corner, and the
figurehead already sees it.

No-one here can lift the softly fallen inevitable, then
none of them can speak with the rage it takes even
to touch coquettish sincerity and in the shade of this fact
my attitude rests on the pillow of the prow of your
neck, prisoner to my bathroom routine, waking

continuously to the same slope of hope, arranging
lunch hours in blocks Tom & Jerry would have
blocked and unblocked, and so on, &c., &c.

I think compassion is a good excuse; I later opened
every cupboard looking for the nature of it.
I want the white wind to scorch my cheeks too, in the
darkness of impending heartbreak. In place of
compelling materialism it would be nice if
the sea-spray froze
luminous seeds authentically sad.

Erec & Enide

Said Erec to Enide, the sun burst
down on my sails and gallowing tore
my winnow North.

Said Enide to Erec, I don't know how
to soothe you.

Said Erec to Enide, the airline strikes pulled
holes in my interior liver tissue, and
I daren't touch a drop.

Said Enide to Erec, God has got your
back.

Said Erec to Enide, this cognitive
behavioural therapy has me
in stitches.

Said Enide to Erec, well then
let's cultivate.

Some shadows passed across the
moon. A sad dog scratched itself.
The horse chestnuts bristled. In the
distance, a car alarm was silenced.

Said Erec to Enide, there is no
bounty in the pillar of my heart
where the undead weekend.

Said Enide to Erec, but the garden
oxygen for you.

Said Erec to Enide, Enide you are
my fondest branches and founding
member state, let me coalesce in your
tender.

Said Enide to Erec, we now have
24-hour banks.

Said Erec to Enide,
Enide dozed, & her lips gently
popped as they parted. Erec sat on
the grass, the horse chestnut on his
chest, and the salmon who jumped,
and the curvature of his intense
guilt, his ergonomic fantasy office
and the parameter of his suburb.

A sad dog scratched the
heaven's mist rose
the 24-hour car park
in valour and honest chivalry.

And on Enide's tresses grew.

Said Erec, a perfectly clean
damsel.

Said Erec, consistently haunted by eight-
syllable rhyming couplets.

Said Erec, it feels like
you've gone away.

Three in a Boat

As conjugal as a deep guitar rakes its lawn and gathers
geniality to add like stars to Christmas stars, mister so-and-so
student busker paedophile and such-and-such,
everyone endeared to the lyrics and here for proof—
too true, prove the proof and we are happily.

As happily as a small car strung out in bluebird crotchets
and frisky vowels, the street shone from Beautiful's
forehead, he couldn't have guessed the wet cobbles were
rays of beans and other enchantments, raw-cheeked and
tenuous we all looped the loop and sailed away

on the pale vanishing point, happily, palacial with ice cream,
turret haircuts, ballot papers in our paws.

I think I was enchanted
I think a trashy sweetness took
the leaf as vowel and parted it
for me.

Then a city grew up nude
and whether it was noon at night—
Nobody was concerned with this; nobody
alighted, or in horror stepped into streams
nomadic, or in happiness glazed.
The Bees—became as Butterflies—
Endless sophisticated Blue
tailed off where the American woman
escalated to shop herself the skies
that Nature murmured to herself,
and murmured, and the future leant
Down in spaces small and paid us
the worth of our work.
The Days—to Mighty Metres stept—
the girls landed on my chest
my chest buckled under set milk and I
Saw backwards through my own eyes.
I could not have defined the change—
wound in light, impeccable constraint
cuffed in happy buggies on the
high street, that bastard we invoked
'Twas a Divine Insanity
But where was the wind, Emily
Where are you gone on the
plate glass where culture smeared its opposite
to tomes of solid Witchcraft—

and where you are incredulous

                    I am under the icing

and where you are the weirdest

                    company I fill the saddest tunes.

Sonnet

I believe a readable face as crickets
swallow gleaming buildings full of
living banking hearts,
I believe the grand ineloquence of
summer's glue talking to you as if
pink axes in our reach,
and you, a click-clack landscape now
your thundering hero-organs chime
a way into my laundry tub.
I believe I'm down with this for shit
is all we have to do to make our
cobbled lottery love
a project with no truth to bear, light-
ness of touch I haven't got

the calm and lovely air.

A Note on Clarity
for Jonathan Tiplady

I pictured a walk in my head, you [were] in it, with pastiches
of [dogs], even grass and loves. I was reckless—I pictured a
walk: kinder people waved from Morris Minors, toast fell out
of kitchens, wood-smoke carried over from distant poems, the
kind this ridicule no [longer] warrants, no warrants, because
there is no policing on this underground sewn into the sky
and the velocity you're made of. Forty comely portraits of you,
Fifty ways to amend my face that I don't have to do, I once
wanted a hot rock white swan but I have none of this in me.
I have none of this in me. And as the plates of earth move [I
don't do it] the London Eye moves and I move in your own
eyes and you do it. How do you do [it], how do you shower
by those pretty boats, knowing the plot of your own movie
and what happens next, knowing everything: Sixty ways to
amend my life, Seventy big lights in the world and looking
surprisingly innocent.

So when there was light in my eyes I was weather,
and I wondered what I could give you.

Then we said the breakthrough was common to both of us
And your hands were presocial.

Then in the commonest form of living I found relief
And your addictions were no longer precious.

I thought clarity had begun.

& since I love the inexact and ideological,

& since this is the only thing that counts,

& since there was never really a poet but a person—

David

David the denoted and substantially
Annotated man. David, I didn't mean
The inconvenient relaying of all we
Had shared to end on a luggage belt
To Italy. David, stop the ride. I want
To get off. For 23 Englishmen and
1 Italian irreversibly imploded I would
Have guaranteed all my love. David
Row into a battleship. David for Unicef.
David the bravest chicken there is. A
Man obscure and B sharp. Sympathy
Forever for living in a wheelchair, the man
Who on reaching critical mass is shot
Out of a Mossberg 12ga. and into my
Mouth. David leaves my mouth
Sedated but soon he rocks down
To the Costcutter to buy beans.
David, reign in your keynote speech
At the Costcutter. David made of
Oak. David diamond.

Five Exits

1

DREAM

In the tunnel of love we felt your
wandering hands and echoes and
we recorded it in real-time gloom.

I learnt nothing from my dream, in
which a bell tower rose from the centre
of a river spotted with flamingoes.

2

SEXUALITY

Though she knows that pimps are scum,
Boxcar takes on a pimp to know
what only pimps know though she knows
that pimps are scum!

A display of poetic justice
asserts the irony of clarity.
I feel as old as Madonna.
So let me be clear.

3

FANTASY

Is 'disgusting' warranted, hardly ever.
I just came here to buy a new pair
of harem pants and I do not share your
hatred, which posits me as lovable.

≈

And I only wrote in condos of prose,
draft text messages and running
spirit and I dreamt only of you.

So many miles beyond 'nice'

4

IMAGINATION

I'm wondering how much money
the patrons of this restaurant own.
I let the Thames write itself, and let you
be fame's pervert.

Stranger, it's a hunger I'm looking for.

5

ART

I have been selfish and sought solace
in the poem that made me businesslike,
I have been businesslike and sought solace
in the poem,

what I write is true, you are
the feather in my hat,
you are the first answer
engulfing my house, you make
a holiday in my heart.

Since We've Lived Here

Consider me in three second shots
on the edges of every Sicilian quarter,
attend to me even through cramp.
If I had practiced reticence
in the face of wet warm and lucid,
looked sideways as beating muscle taught
in glades of basking, gold-thieving

I would never have. And if
I grew old it was only because I
was cooing the corn down after
the show and did not forget you
dusk, hassled you down too, to the
last damp thread to separate my calf
in the milky goo. Allow me

to descend in a force field around
your fecund head, plush don't
worry since I fret for the both of us,
Erec & Enide, I spite you in return
and forget my curiosity for the unseen
notebooks and strap my hair in difficult
positions 'til I cannot go outside, cannot.

Regard me as your honey bee
in primary colours, paint my toes in
shades of your mother's living room,
revisit your childhood, make me your mother,
like a dove startled out of the cave
in the secret honeycombs of the rock
I came out astonished and awry.

[23]

Consider me in your kind of place where
the critical vocabulary belongs to our
castle in the middle distance,
appraise me in a scandalous dressing-down
of rubric and feel me up in the toilets,
a seductive submissive ingénue, and am
I that name.

One Two

Big dusk, where you flattered the old trees
so 'til little dogs lead dog-lives like dogs
in your kindness, wild posies levitate in my
arms unbunched, and here on our bench
we are me and you lover of puzzles.

Lover, happy to fabulate with each other,
glad to sypher the lanes down between the
hot air where picnickers sat, drawn to the
soul-bruise and gaudy trunks, under a dead
sea I know the answer is a rich, friable soil.

Tell me how your harmony with nature
evolved into your harmony with information
technology. Was it a condition of eternal
hypocrisy or was it a moral image of thought
reducing my two tits to an error?

Rueful colours of the animal sphere,
scenic holidays with you, one two,
Older Lover, the many-tiered missives
great deciding battles between hands and
feet and huge men felled in wake of you.

Lisa Jarnot's Rabbit

after Lisa Jarnot

How to glide on promise
hunted hunted honed the sky
alone lacking ground a sky
alone on the border of a shadow
of a cloud betrothed and hunted
down,

How to sleeping number honed
and died the ground a felt a
tear that landed on the border
of a cloud in promised hand who
flew alone in hunted tones and
gliding hunted honed,

Near to hunters weeping warned
a shadow promised hungry
bowed and fur tucked back to warn
the sleeping hunters of the
rabbit flown on gliding promise boned
and full of womb,

Near to sleeping gliders stowed
the Federation huge and bored,
wasteful loomed and fully trash
and stoned below the tear
in unwound lacking towns and
borders hunking low,

How to die asleep on
lacking, lacking cascade globe
all bored to death open and tuned
to gliding rabbit worn of sky
and worn of sleep and skin and Pleiades'
reckoned furry crown,

Reckoned secret furry stash
and rolling promise owned
hereby the woolly rabbit leapt
a crescent over the town
and hunted hunted hunted
rabbit live a-thumping honed.

Letter to John Clare

Do you mind about the revision of global brightening
or me —
If I insist the inverse of the phrase I choose to fell?

Do you want me to undo it for you, and do you want
to be mesmerised by first principles,

Or tarred film, or would you like me to tell you a story
from the future, a rare antiquity fashioned by decisions
gone back on?

Do you want to talk down a street or a slope?
The idea of stunning plants for beauty doesn't choke
like a great person.
I needed folded times.

You are a great person —
The orchid of the internet. Do you
mind if I don't come with you is it very

Highlighted live or pre-recorded? Is it fallow?

Do you want liquid tablets or snowy powder to fall upon: now then

tell me how long the epiphany takes, so that I,

I wonder

do you mind about how reservations are made for you

then slide from you.

I needed to be unfelt and shrug it off.

It's false that youth is more robust and bounces with

the seasons, but

Did you want me as a living sea or waking dream,

a huge shipwreck to be awfully afraid of tho not terrified,

a little ferocity in bloom?

I know,

you are gone somewhere concave then convex.

I know this

because the wind straight through my chest.

Do you like to set the tone—

Could you ever say, *so it may be said of dreams*, against anomie,

for revelation, over email, with commensurate effort.

Lena at the Beach

In the blossom of the brain, in so far as I am people,
in terms of my churlishness in the context of a lowering
sky of lifestyle, being a person moreover, being a person
takeover, in identifying people it helps to consider a
person a salty brick, the lusty exposition left of a person
leftover alongside sheepish person subjects in any
rearticulation of a person the people are on dodgy
ground, in misreading the script of being beauty I was
black beauty and a womaniser.

Who cares about the psychosocial fabrications of a lusty brick?

What if it's wrong?

What if I want to lie, compete, ease my conscience on a salty brick?

Rest my hot cheek pearling beads of salt onto the
perverse orange brick of saturated consolation with
radical implications for all girls and boys who dare to be
churlish, who forget the brick and blossom of my body
and remember to speak through the irony of
windbreakers broken by the wind and tossed to sea in
the bedroom where no one has sex.

≈

In the paranoid Huguenot daughter, in our margins we
love to be lofty, in my heart-thumping under scudding
clouds in my stomach when I think about it, in grouchy
thickets and bark's little teeth I'm again a Swedish
model looking over my shoulder at November 1972.

Arriving at the beach in the context of a coveting
style of life, in the scrubby bench I found again
my teeth,

I bit to chew and chewed hard to make it known
that I am not here for smiling, coyness, shyness, or was
it something I had in mind grinning growling yakking
making my presence felt or manning up, I was too
young for algorithms,

to be spewing myself out of windows off bridges in front of tube trains,
did I never want to learn poetry brick, no no!
I wanted only to write programs and lie down bucolic.

I lay in the sand and the dead moved over me, his long hair
lapped my leg and my oily sun cream and my Katrina,
my Santa Ana, I learned your names less subject-to-error
you move rapidly northward less I lose you all.

≈

Give me your name.
Roll me down through a name's universal blue river
and give me.
Your name was not a gift but a given.

Donated Anita of stainless steel and Tetra Pak,
there is more truth in you, Anita of kulturlos I applaud your cunning.

At the historical moment of your inception you were coming.

At the unconscious hill of habit.

∼

In the comfort of the taking, to the extent the dead
men. However they died to me. However they sold
their wares on the doorstep on red tiles I saw them
through frosted glass I felt their hot panacean feet.
However I was born.

What penalty might be incurred
for succumbing?
Categorical uselessness
or my bucket of sand.

I grew boldly in their raunchy village, and wept frequently.

I rode home on several bicycles, I was ridden of doubt.

My little empire glowered.

Soliloquy for Living People

Retreat now is brave and wide so
a demand to be taken seriously
falters clean off the ramparts
of articulate laws and this trans-
figures, too, to sicky wanness
in the department as it continues
forgetting you,
and it turns out that it's back here in
the country where the contingent
chorus is hidden, an unlikely suspect,
clearly we are no longer seductive in our
flaying but dying to careen down
that circumscribed crevice where no
man had been, or we had been, the
kind of backstage we had been
wanting, and bound to be tied thereby,
I could never speak.

But the point of privilege must be
to watch cars skid slowly and clamp
the motor of our tongues until
we learn the value of cultural aphasia
within our sense of having gotten somewhere,

for this 'I' that you read:

any place on the colours of a fishing line
towed down a dual carriageway to which
we do not belong,

any place between the stripes of a bright carton into which
I could be lowered ceremoniously,

any place within some international community
existing for the purpose of condoning its own
shallow breathing,

any place in which my non-existing daughter
may through colour know her own womb,

any place in which I and my daughter
may know, a place every day I fail to know
it well enough—

Jaguar

And now the funeral directors have taken you away
in long grasses,
though you are not dead, and you are not a discarded
home beat room door shape soap
on the corner of my tongue, by sonic triptychs
I am only going down Essex Road,
I am humaner today
than yesterday
when I did not grasp the last poem,

the very last poem ever written,

but I did grasp it, and

you were on target, and as the pinnacle rose
I was wandering among many when my enamel burst
like windows do, broke into luxury sopranos
and there you were—

reading Donne through the wall.

Notes

1. *'Thou art my hope O Lord God*
   Thou was my truſt in my Youth'
— Inscribed on the tomb of Thomas, son of Isaac Nevill
   Gen: by Sarah his wife, who died the 12th May 1744, aged
   16 years. (Lavenham Church, Suffolk)

2. *'That the Joy will soon come and make you suffer!'*
— Chrétien De Troyes, *Erec and Enide*. Trans. Carleton W.
   Carroll. Penguin, 2004.

3. Lines from Emily Dickinson's '593':
'I think I was enchanted'
'and whether it was noon at night —'
'The Bees — became as Butterflies —'
'that Nature murmured to herself,'
'The Days — to Mighty Metres stept —'
'I could not have defined the change —'
''Twas a Divine Insanity'
'to tomes of solid Witchcraft —'
— *The Complete Poems of Emily Dickinson*. Thomas H. Johnson (ed.).
   Little, Brown, & Company, 1988.

4. *Like a dove startled out of the cave*
— Virgil, *The Aeneid*. Trans. David West. Penguin, 2003.

5. *'so it may be said of dreams'*
— John Clare, 'A Remarkable Dream'. *John Clare by Himself*. Eric
   Robinson and David Powell (eds.). Fyfield Books, 1996.

www.ingramcontent.com/pod-product-compliance
Lightning Source LLC
Chambersburg PA
CBHW061159040426

42445CB00013B/1745